Sense Your Feelings

Julieanne Schaller

BALBOA.PRESS

A DIVISION OF HAY HOUSE

Balboa Press books may be ordered through booksellers or by contacting:

Balboa Press
A Division of Hay House
1663 Liberty Drive
Bloomington, IN 47403
www.balboapress.com
844-682-1282

ISBN: 979-8-7652-3989-6 (sc)
ISBN: 979-8-7652-3990-2 (e)

Print information available on the last page.

Balboa Press rev. date: 03/31/2023

If your feeling had a SOUND what would it be?

What would it SMELL like?

What would it TASTE like?

What would it feel like if you could TOUCH it?

What COLOR is your feeling?
Does it have a SHAPE?
What SIZE is it?

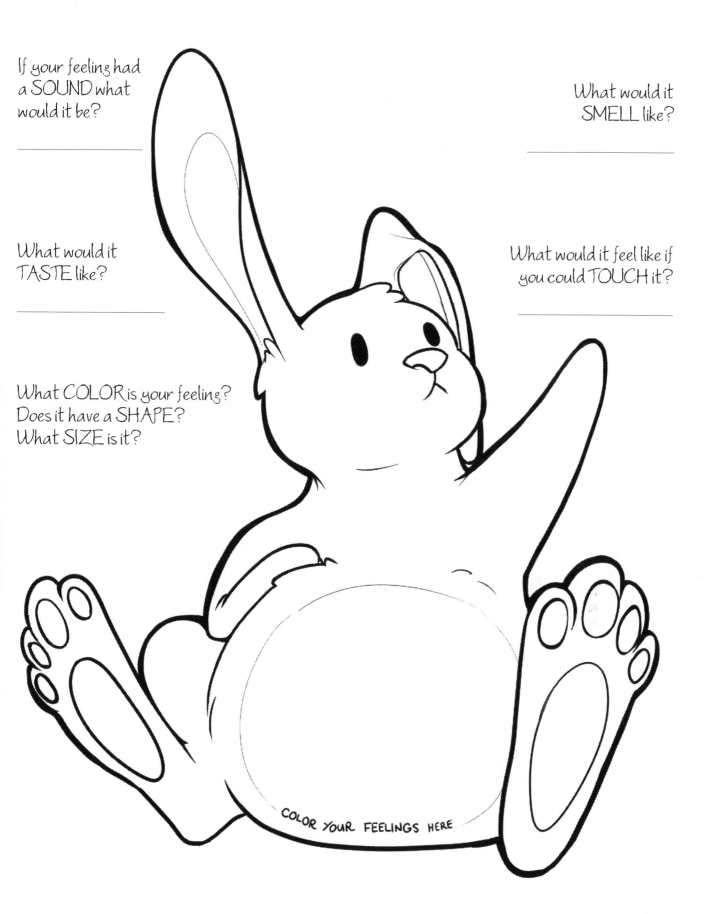

COLOR YOUR FEELINGS HERE

Use another page to color how you wish you felt

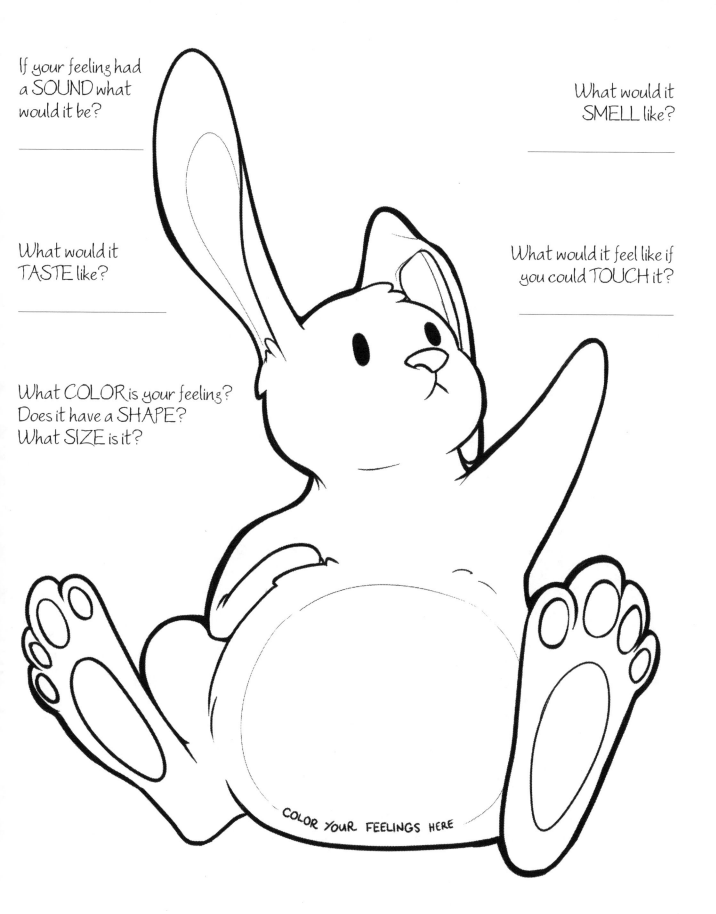

If your feeling had a SOUND what would it be?

What would it SMELL like?

What would it TASTE like?

What would it feel like if you could TOUCH it?

What COLOR is your feeling? Does it have a SHAPE? What SIZE is it?

COLOR YOUR FEELINGS HERE

Use another page to color how you wish you felt

If your feeling had a SOUND what would it be?

What would it SMELL like?

What would it TASTE like?

What would it feel like if you could TOUCH it?

What COLOR is your feeling? Does it have a SHAPE? What SIZE is it?

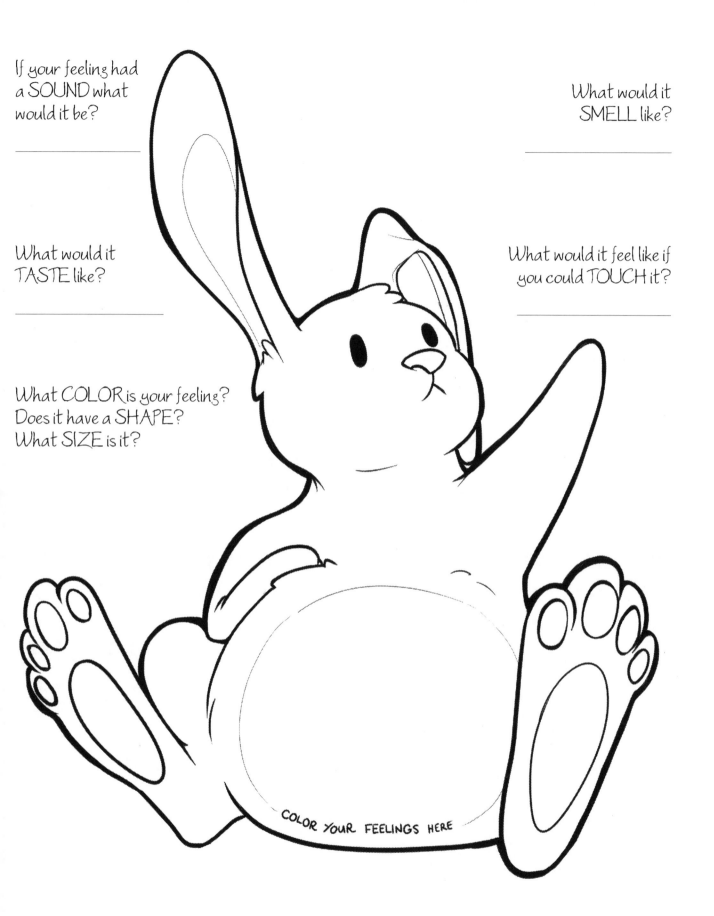

COLOR YOUR FEELINGS HERE

Use another page to color how you wish you felt

If your feeling had a SOUND what would it be?

What would it SMELL like?

What would it TASTE like?

What would it feel like if you could TOUCH it?

What COLOR is your feeling?
Does it have a SHAPE?
What SIZE is it?

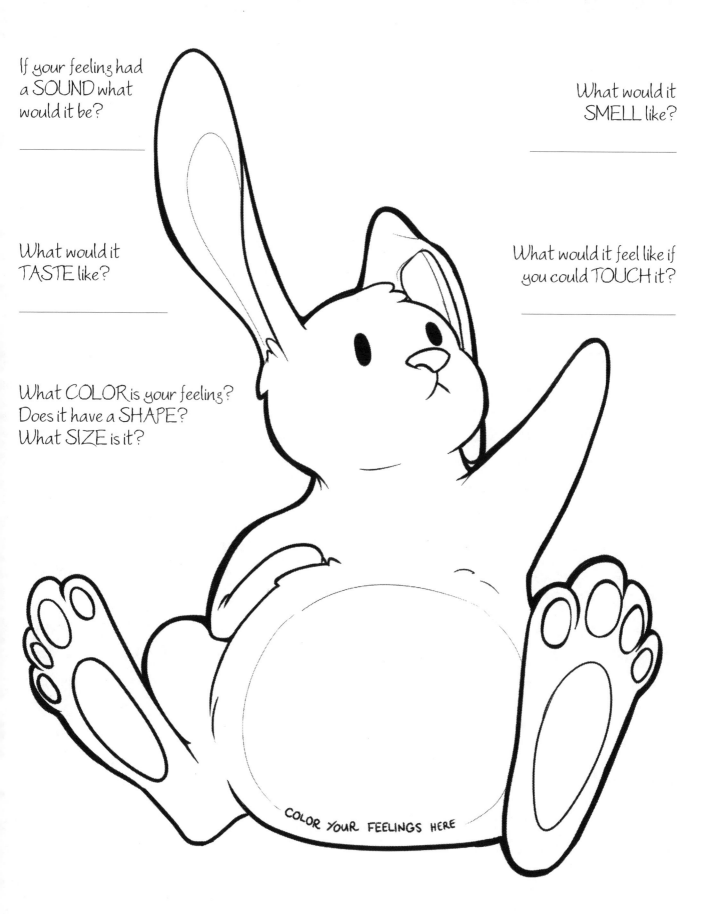

COLOR YOUR FEELINGS HERE

Use another page to color how you wish you felt

If your feeling had a SOUND what would it be?

_____

What would it TASTE like?

_____

What COLOR is your feeling?
Does it have a SHAPE?
What SIZE is it?

What would it SMELL like?

_____

What would it feel like if you could TOUCH it?

_____

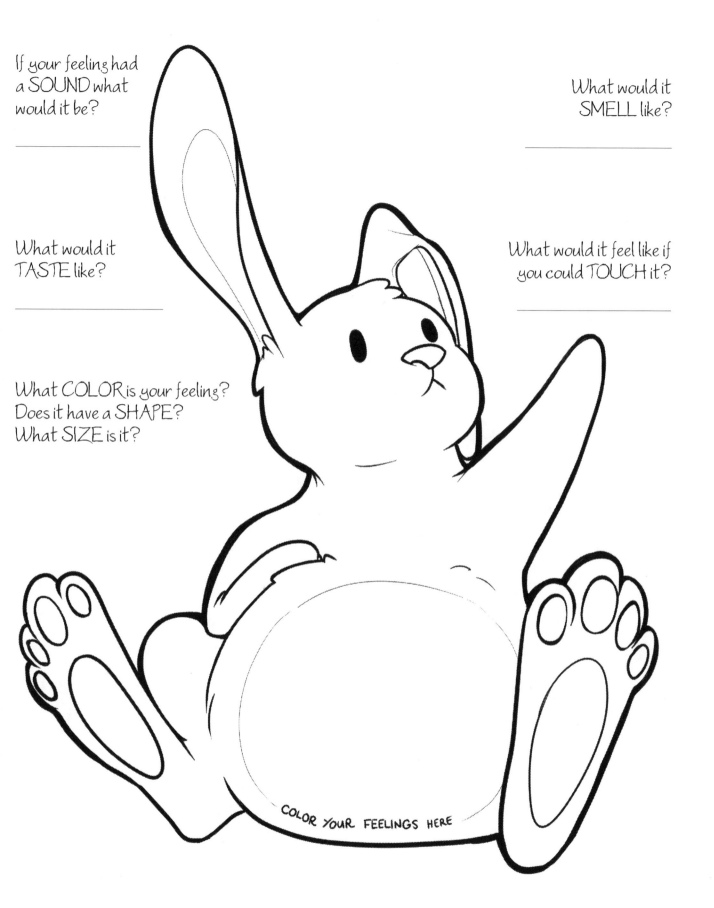

COLOR YOUR FEELINGS HERE

Use another page to color how you wish you felt

If your feeling had a SOUND what would it be?

What would it SMELL like?

What would it TASTE like?

What would it feel like if you could TOUCH it?

What COLOR is your feeling?
Does it have a SHAPE?
What SIZE is it?

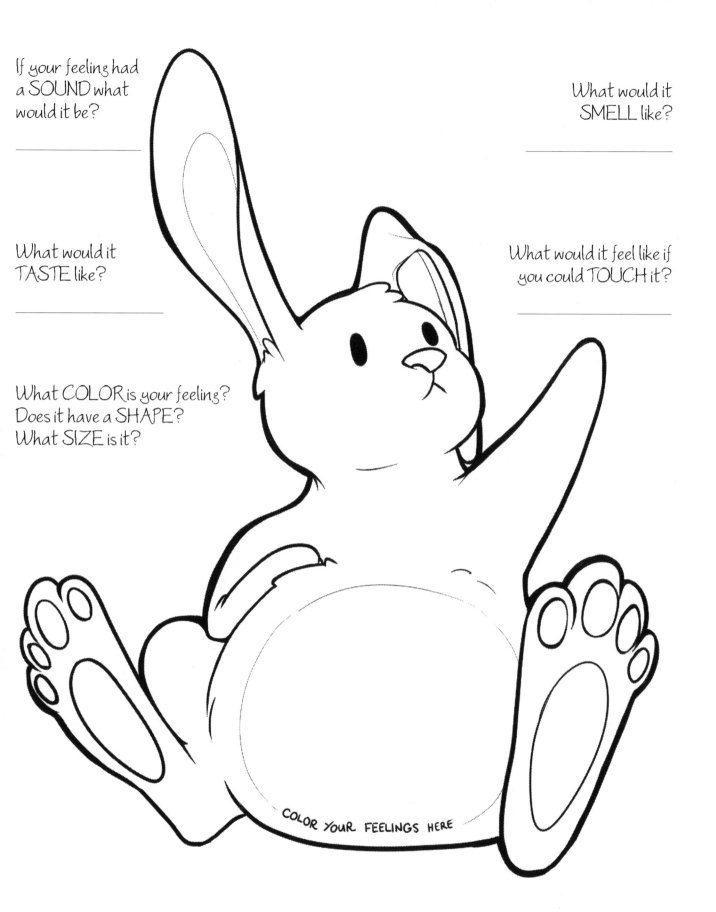

COLOR YOUR FEELINGS HERE

Use another page to color how you wish you felt

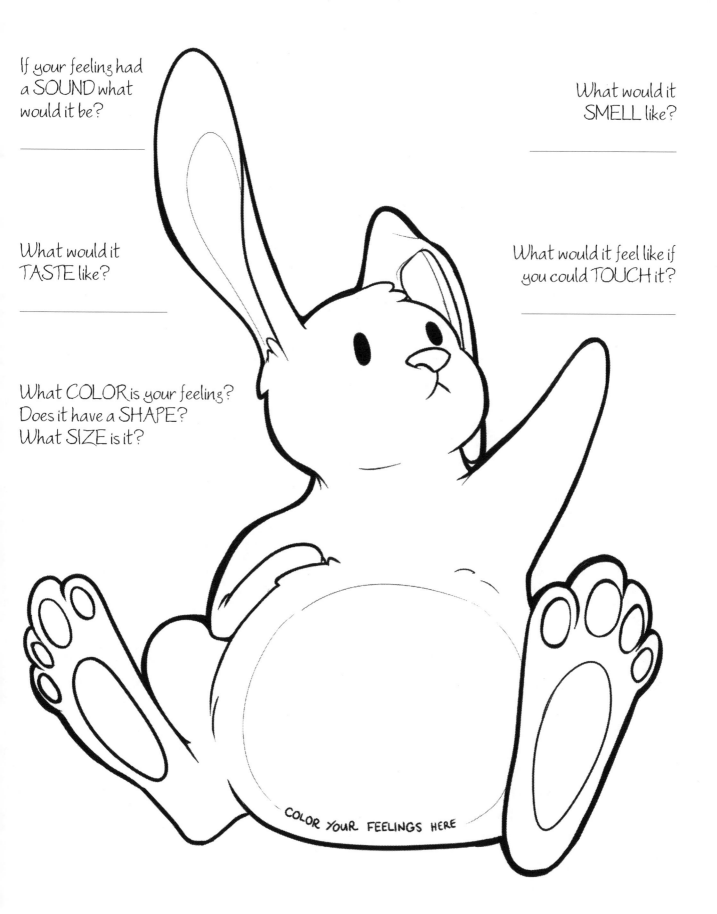

If your feeling had a SOUND what would it be?

What would it SMELL like?

What would it TASTE like?

What would it feel like if you could TOUCH it?

What COLOR is your feeling?
Does it have a SHAPE?
What SIZE is it?

COLOR YOUR FEELINGS HERE

Use another page to color how you wish you felt

If your feeling had a SOUND what would it be?

What would it SMELL like?

What would it TASTE like?

What would it feel like if you could TOUCH it?

What COLOR is your feeling? Does it have a SHAPE? What SIZE is it?

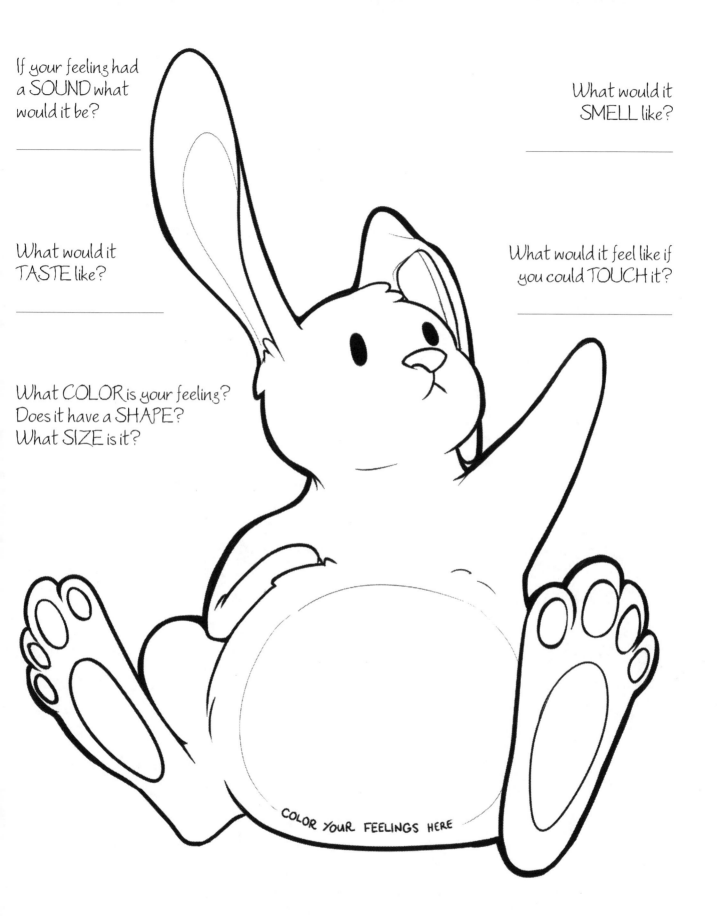

COLOR YOUR FEELINGS HERE

Use another page to color how you wish you felt

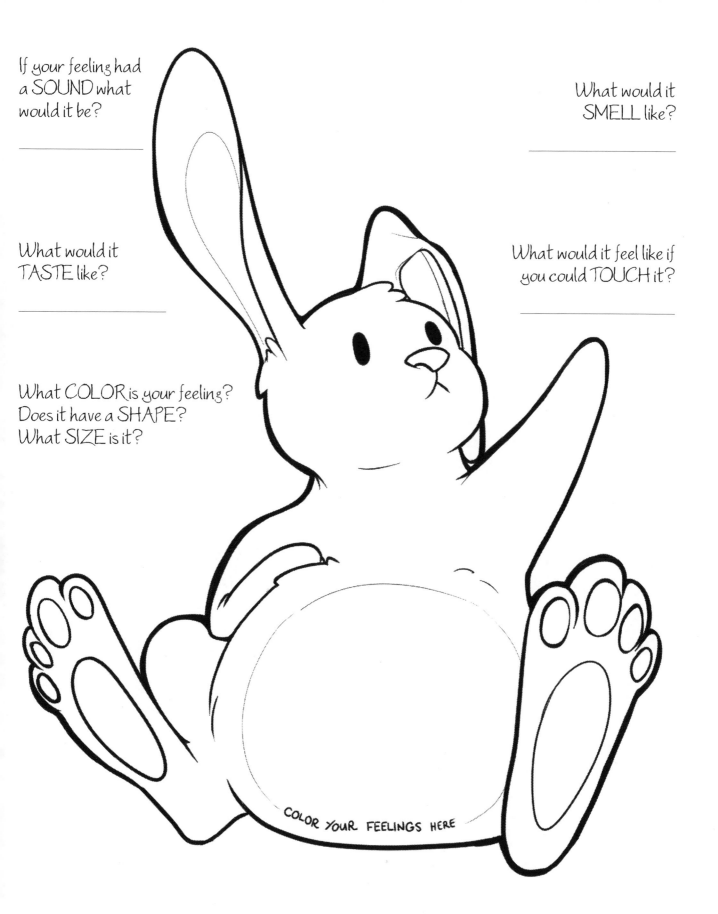

If your feeling had a SOUND what would it be?

What would it SMELL like?

What would it TASTE like?

What would it feel like if you could TOUCH it?

What COLOR is your feeling? Does it have a SHAPE? What SIZE is it?

COLOR YOUR FEELINGS HERE

Use another page to color how you wish you felt

If your feeling had a SOUND what would it be?

What would it SMELL like?

What would it TASTE like?

What would it feel like if you could TOUCH it?

What COLOR is your feeling? Does it have a SHAPE? What SIZE is it?

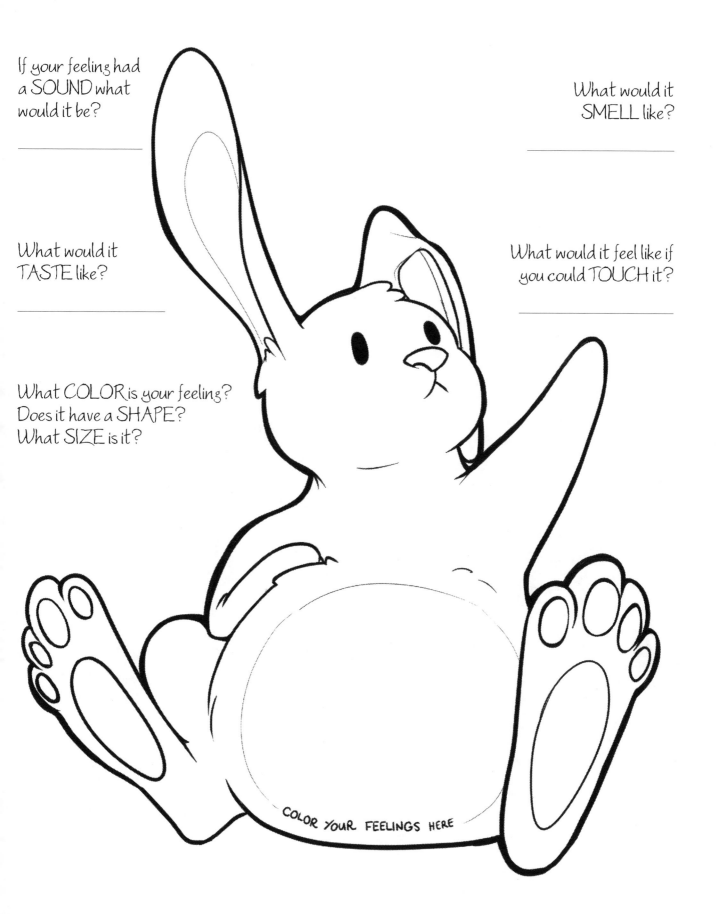

COLOR YOUR FEELINGS HERE

Use another page to color how you wish you felt

If your feeling had a SOUND what would it be?

What would it SMELL like?

What would it TASTE like?

What would it feel like if you could TOUCH it?

What COLOR is your feeling? Does it have a SHAPE? What SIZE is it?

COLOR YOUR FEELINGS HERE

Use another page to color how you wish you felt

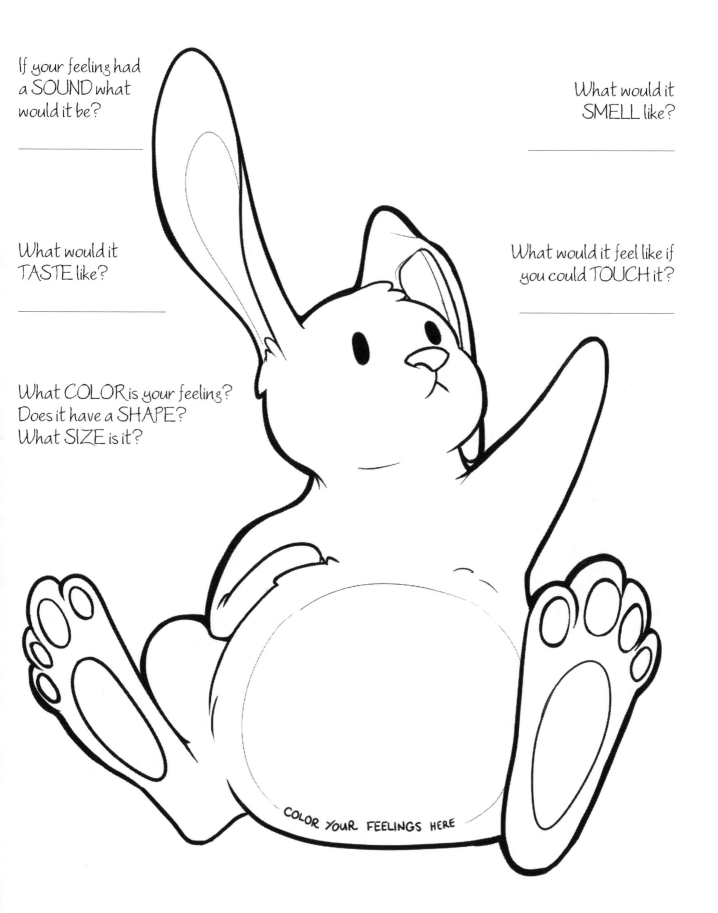

If your feeling had a SOUND what would it be?

What would it SMELL like?

What would it TASTE like?

What would it feel like if you could TOUCH it?

What COLOR is your feeling? Does it have a SHAPE? What SIZE is it?

COLOR YOUR FEELINGS HERE

Use another page to color how you wish you felt

If your feeling had a SOUND what would it be?

What would it SMELL like?

What would it TASTE like?

What would it feel like if you could TOUCH it?

What COLOR is your feeling? Does it have a SHAPE? What SIZE is it?

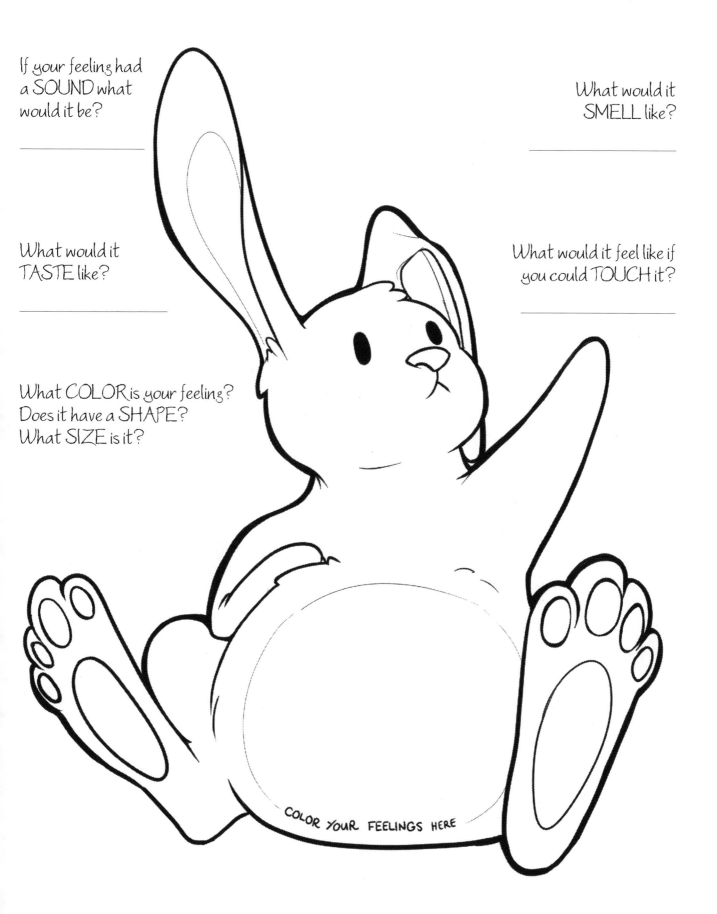

COLOR YOUR FEELINGS HERE

Use another page to color how you wish you felt

If your feeling had a SOUND what would it be?

What would it SMELL like?

What would it TASTE like?

What would it feel like if you could TOUCH it?

What COLOR is your feeling? Does it have a SHAPE? What SIZE is it?

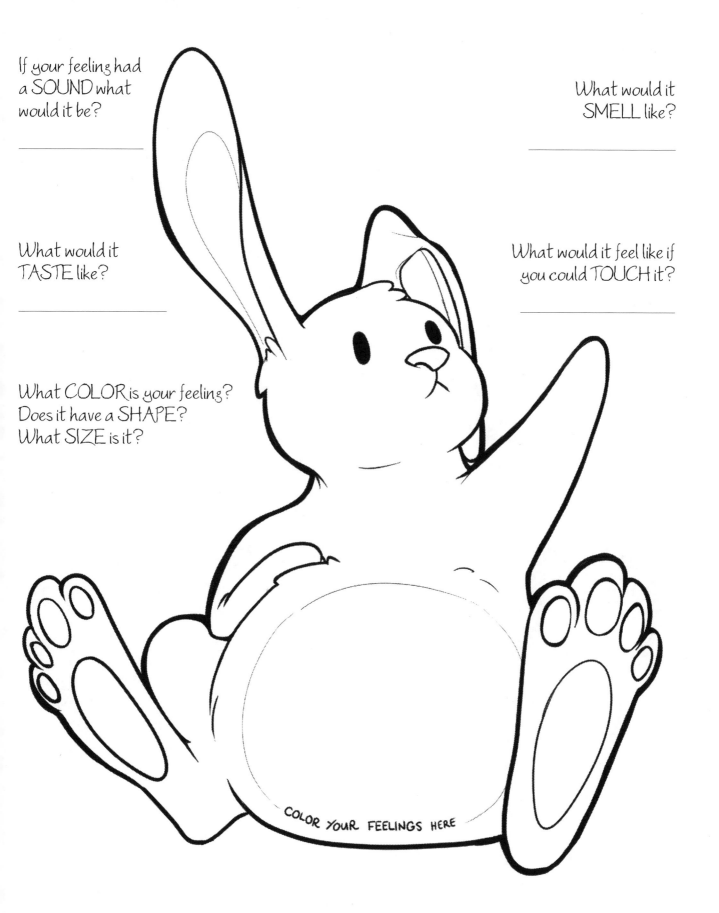

COLOR YOUR FEELINGS HERE

Use another page to color how you wish you felt

If your feeling had a SOUND what would it be?

What would it SMELL like?

What would it TASTE like?

What would it feel like if you could TOUCH it?

What COLOR is your feeling? Does it have a SHAPE? What SIZE is it?

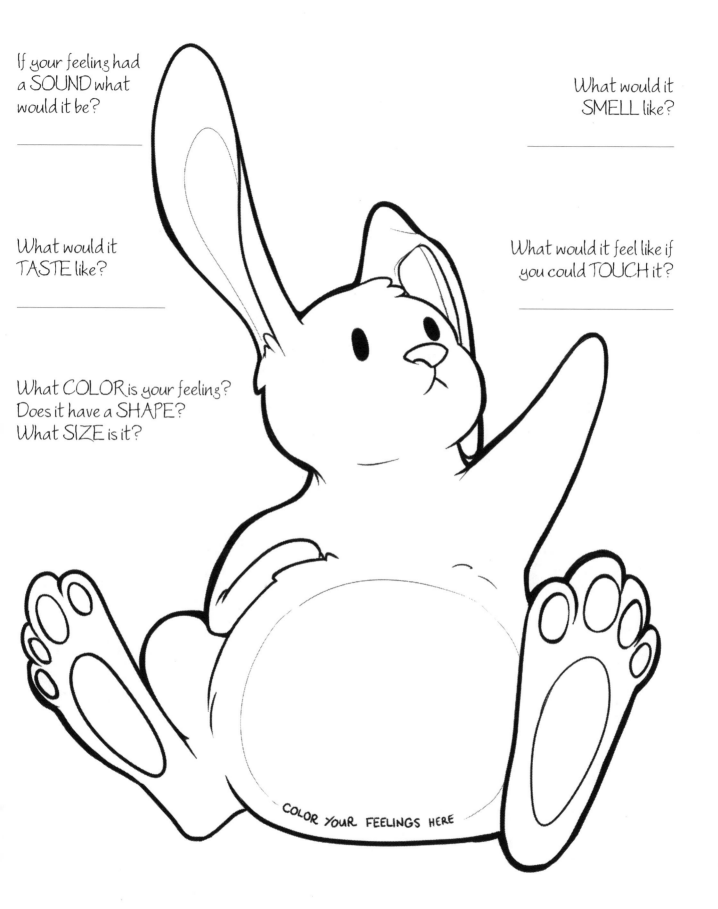

COLOR YOUR FEELINGS HERE

Use another page to color how you wish you felt

If your feeling had a SOUND what would it be?

What would it SMELL like?

What would it TASTE like?

What would it feel like if you could TOUCH it?

What COLOR is your feeling?
Does it have a SHAPE?
What SIZE is it?

COLOR YOUR FEELINGS HERE

Use another page to color how you wish you felt

If your feeling had a SOUND what would it be?

What would it SMELL like?

What would it TASTE like?

What would it feel like if you could TOUCH it?

What COLOR is your feeling?
Does it have a SHAPE?
What SIZE is it?

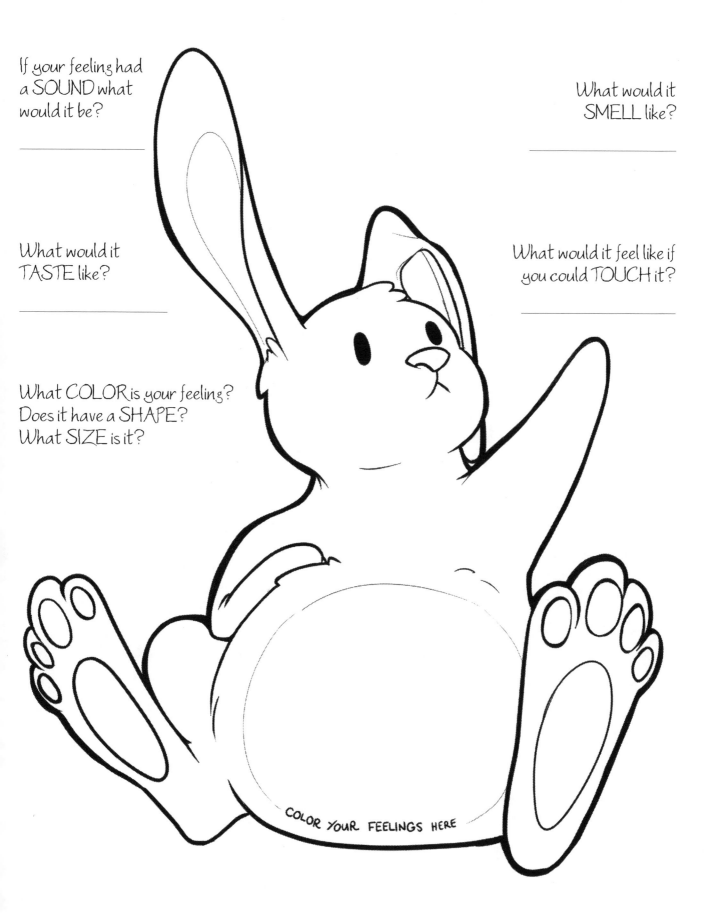

COLOR YOUR FEELINGS HERE

Use another page to color how you wish you felt

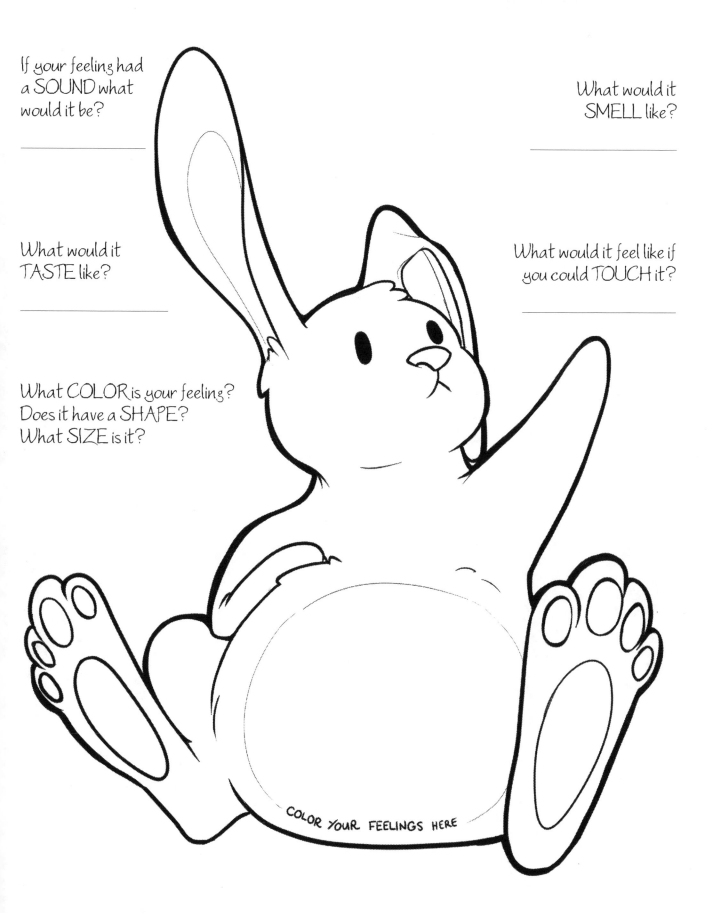

If your feeling had a SOUND what would it be?

What would it SMELL like?

What would it TASTE like?

What would it feel like if you could TOUCH it?

What COLOR is your feeling?
Does it have a SHAPE?
What SIZE is it?

COLOR YOUR FEELINGS HERE

Use another page to color how you wish you felt

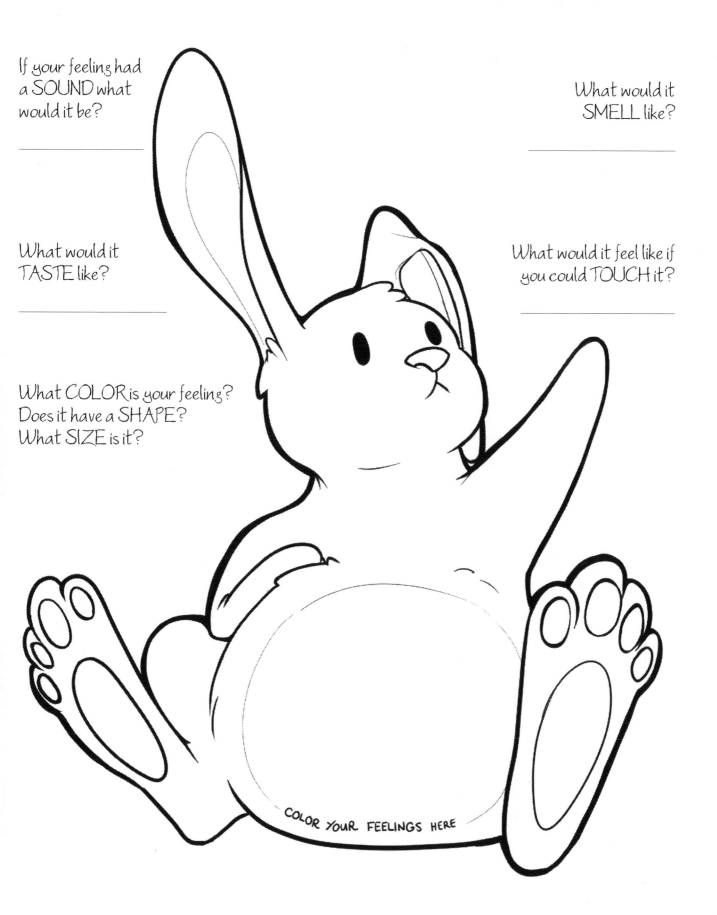

If your feeling had a SOUND what would it be?

What would it SMELL like?

What would it TASTE like?

What would it feel like if you could TOUCH it?

What COLOR is your feeling?
Does it have a SHAPE?
What SIZE is it?

COLOR YOUR FEELINGS HERE

Use another page to color how you wish you felt

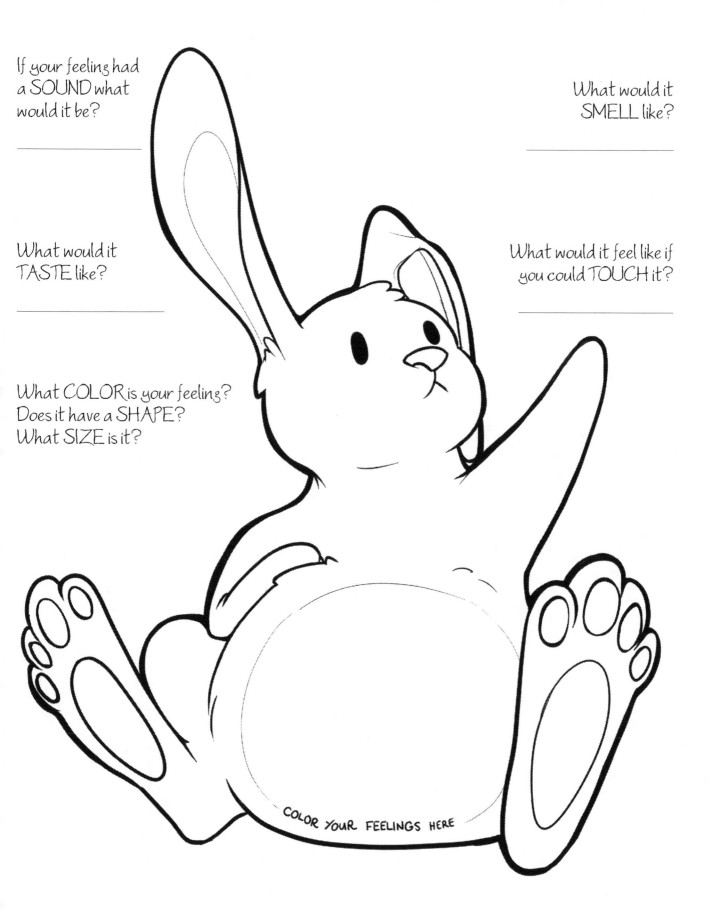

If your feeling had a SOUND what would it be?

What would it SMELL like?

What would it TASTE like?

What would it feel like if you could TOUCH it?

What COLOR is your feeling? Does it have a SHAPE? What SIZE is it?

COLOR YOUR FEELINGS HERE

Use another page to color how you wish you felt

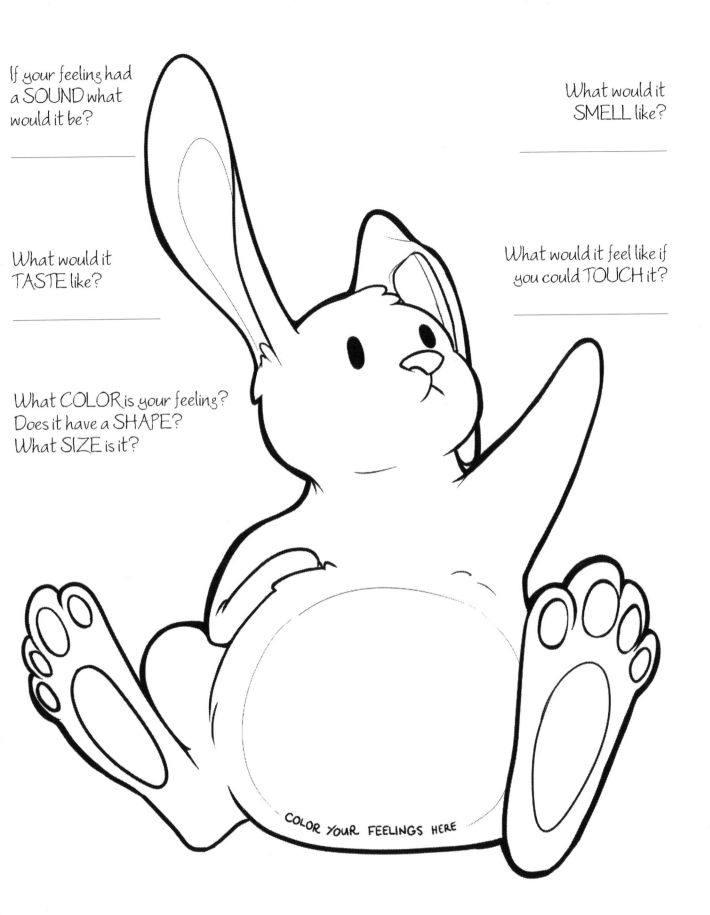

If your feeling had a SOUND what would it be?

What would it SMELL like?

What would it TASTE like?

What would it feel like if you could TOUCH it?

What COLOR is your feeling?
Does it have a SHAPE?
What SIZE is it?

COLOR YOUR FEELINGS HERE

Use another page to color how you wish you felt

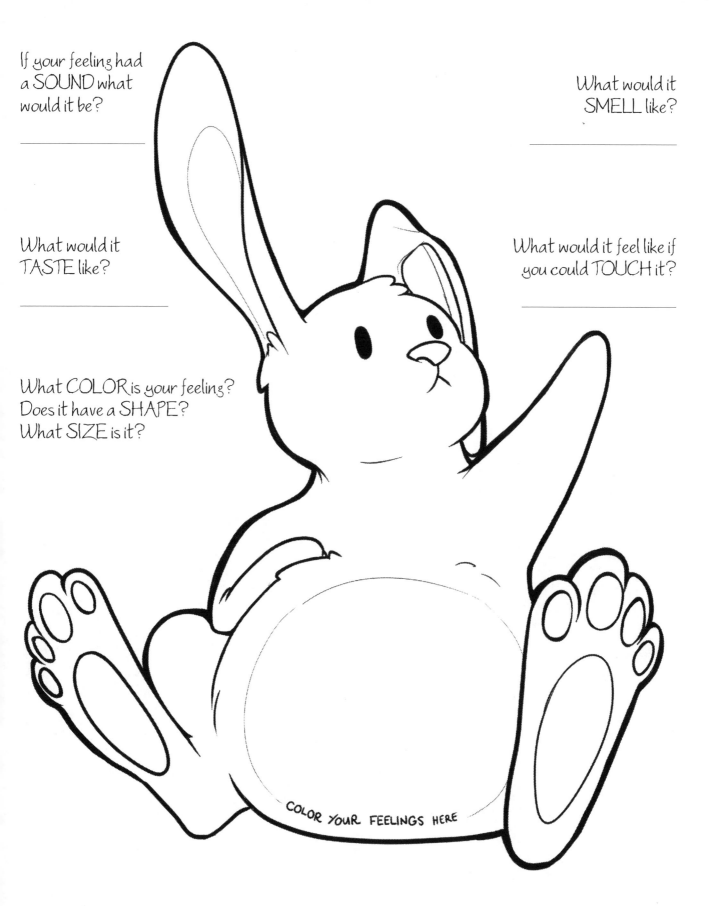

If your feeling had a SOUND what would it be?

What would it SMELL like?

What would it TASTE like?

What would it feel like if you could TOUCH it?

What COLOR is your feeling? Does it have a SHAPE? What SIZE is it?

COLOR YOUR FEELINGS HERE

Use another page to color how you wish you felt

Printed in the United States
by Baker & Taylor Publisher Services